LETTERS TO
THE EDITOR

Printed in the United States of America.

ISBN 978-0-9970242-9-6

J Winthrop, Charleston, South Carolina

www.winthropfamily.org

DEDICATION

To Ben Long, English teacher at Buckley School in the 1940s.
He gave us the inspiration as well as some of the tools to
try our hand at writing.

TABLE OF CONTENTS

INTRODUCTION

Over the years my urge to write has been channeled in different directions - creating a newspaper for a unit of the U. S. Navy, publishing op-ed items for a variety of newspapers, and contributing articles to magazines.

Having settled in Charleston, S. C., in the 1990s, however, nearly all written material was intended for the family and/or friends. The only articles submitted for public consumption took the form of letters to the editor of the local paper - *The Post & Courier*.

An imperfect effort has been made to arrange most of these letters as they appeared in chronological order.

J.W.

The Post and Courier

Thursday, December 16, 1993

Son unlike father

The visit of Dr. Sergei Kruschchev to Charleston was a memorable event — particularly for those of us who visited the Soviet Union during his father's rule. While he resembles his father, his manner was warm and gentle. It seemed appropriate in a way to have our lovely city, the Holy City, welcome this visiting senior fellow from Brown University and to learn from him.

We have come a long way from the time when his father banged his shoe on the table in New York.

JOHN WINTHROP
1 NORTH ADGER'S WHARF

The Post and Courier

Sunday, February 6, 1994, Letters to the Editor

Historic flight

The Bush-Yeltsin agreement to harness United States and Russian space efforts jointly paid a big dividend early on the morning of February 3.

Sergei Kirkalev joined five American astronauts in the launching of the space shuttle Discovery.

As guests of NASA and NUI, a gas utility holding company providing energy to the Space Center, we were allowed to talk to cosmonauts and to witness the event from a prime location.

Shortly after sunrise the spacecraft thundered into the blue sky. Moments later, the earth trembled and all of us knew we had witnessed an historic event — a spectacular achievement.

One could hope, for that one brief shining moment at least, that there might be grounds for considering more U.S.-Russian cooperation on many fronts.

As we departed the viewing stand, we knew the five Americans and the Russian could see no boundaries between nations as they look down at the earth.

The overwhelming logic of more energetic cooperation as we tackle scientific and environmental and space problems might just win the day.

Thank you George Bush, and thank you Boris Yeltsin for giving our space effort a new dimension. My wife and I returned home to Charleston very inspired and very grateful.

JOHN WINTHROP
1 NORTH ADGER'S WHARF

14

The Post and Courier

Friday, May 13, 1994, Letters to the Editor

Croatian dignitaries

For most of us, our only knowledge of Croatia is based upon the war which continues to rage in the former Yugoslavia.

It is a little known fact, however, that the Croatian city of Dubrovnik was the first city-state to recognize the United States as an independent country and the original stones which built the White House are from Croatia.

This historical link continues to grow. This past week, the city of Charleston hosted the visit of four Croatian dignitaries: Nikola Obuljen, Josko Belamaric, Jadran Antolovic and Ivan Saric.

These names are not as familiar as John C. Calhoun and Francis Marion to us, but their jobs are of consequence — The Lord Mayor of Dubrovnik, Conservator of Cultural Monuments, Deputy Minister for International Cultural Exchange and General Secretary of the Ministry of Education and Culture.

This trip was more than a mission of good will.

With sponsorship from the Charleston Area Council for International Development, a division of the South Carolina World Trade Center and the State Department, these leading citizens from Croatia came to Charleston to learn how we protect and preserve our historic treasures, our buildings and our artifacts. They were welcomed by the Rotary Club and others.

Charleston made a powerful impression on these fine people. Moreover, we have been reminded once again that the work of the Historic Charleston Foundation is of national, indeed global, significance.

JOHN WINTHROP
1 NORTH ADGER'S WHARF

The Post and Courier

Monday, July 18, 1994, Letters to the Editor

Treasure in trees

As a tree farmer for the past 30 years, I was pleased to see your recent lead editorial on the need to increase this resource. Trees provide shelter for wildlife, protect soil from wind erosion, purify the air and beautify our state.

A planter of trees can create a good business and develop a perpetual yield here in the "timber basket." Income can be supplemented with hunting-right's payments and/or cabin rental on a property of moderate size.

The planter of trees can receive psychic benefits while improving the environment and lining the pocketbook. You're on the "side of the angels" when you educate us about the need for more trees.

JOHN WINTHROP
1 NORTH ADGER'S WHARF

16

The Post and Courier

date unknown, Letters to the Editor

Great bridge day

What a splendid event the Cooper River Walk/Run was for Charleston! It combined all the elements of good exercise, good fellowship and a good boost to the local economy.

For me it provided yet another dividend. At the last minute I registered my son, Teddy, as well as myself. (Teddy is almost exactly 50 years younger than his aging father.) He showed immediate enthusiasm for the idea and sprang from his bed early on the morning of March 25.

Together we took the bus to the other side of the river with our friend, Rick Little, another resident of Charleston. We suffered a little discomfort from the early morning cold, along with a pain or two while making the hike amidst thousands. But we were not trampled; we were not made to feel diminished by our relatively slow pace.

Together we walked across the bridge. We admired the boats below us, the warming blue sky above, and the cries of encouragement of those along the way.

It was a great day for both of us and a bonding experience we will long remember.

JOHN WINTHROP
1 NORTH ADGER'S WHARF

The Post and Courier

date unknown, Letters to the Editor

Do we have the courage?

Before any time elapses, it seems important to me, as a good Republican, to respond to President Clinton's initiative on attacking the deficit. Clearly, President Bush had the opportunity to focus on this major domestic problem after his triumph with Desert Storm. Many of us were disappointed to see him miss the opportunity — particularly after the Reagan-Bush team had demonstrated success in getting inflation under control during the 1980s.

President Clinton, in my view, has shown some real courage in facing up to the federal deficit, which threatens us as much as nuclear or environmental catastrophe. Now the key question remains: Does he have the courage, and do we have the courage, to make the deep spending cuts which will be required?

If we have the fortitude to cut back in nearly all areas, including entitlements, none of us will mind paying higher taxes to close the deficit.

Generations that follow will be grateful if we swallow both bitter pills: higher taxes and lower spending.

JOHN WINTHROP
1 NORTH ADGER'S WHARF

The Post and Courier

Tuesday, August 30, 1994, Letters to the Editor

The Sanford victory

Republicans and Democrats should pay attention to Mark Sanford's victory. Despite overwhelming odds, Jenny and Mark Sanford made a decision to attack deficit spending in Washington, to avoid the seduction of all special interest groups and to embark on a road of personal and family sacrifice.

Before announcing his candidacy for Congress, Mark Sanford spent considerable time writing a careful position statement on key issues.

In the words of Teddy Roosevelt, he declined the comforts of his heritage and made the decision to step "into the arena."

JOHN WINTHROP
1 NORTH ADGER'S WHARF

The Post and Courier

Economic challenges

What welcome news comes to us from the Northeast!

After many years of economic stagnation, Massachusetts appears to be climbing out of the abyss with new enterprises replacing many of the old ones along Route 128 and elsewhere in that state. Gov. Weld deserves much credit.

By reaching out to the business community, cutting expenses and reducing taxes, he is restoring vitality to his state to such a degree that the story got front page attention in *The New York Times* — hardly a conservative newspaper!

The economy of South Carolina and of Charleston faces a different set of challenges, but we must have confidence in our many attributes — an excellent labor force, a splendid center for shipping, reasonably low taxes, and a great quality of life, among others.

JOHN WINTHROP
1 NORTH ADGER'S WHARF

The Post and Courier

Tuesday, April 25, 1995, Letters to the Editor

Avoiding disaster

Every day we are reminded of the need to cut taxes and balance the budget. We continue to dance around the question of entitlements and Social Security.

It is only after changes and modifications are made in these areas that we can avoid economic disaster on a longer-term basis. We can only hope that the American public can understand this essential fact soon and that our legislators will act.

We are fortunate to have Mark Sanford representing us with an intelligent and supportive wife by his side. I believe the Sanfords understand the issue.

JOHN WINTHROP
1 NORTH ADGER'S WHARF

The Post and Courier

Tuesday, June 27, 1995, Letters to the Editor

Fund a tree

There is something mystical about trees. Human beings have understood the importance of trees — at least subconsciously — since the beginning of time.

We care about trees not just for shelter or firewood or environmental reasons alone, but rather as a basic prerequisite for our quality of life. In our increasingly urban society, this need is felt with more urgency. Trees bring joy and a better environment and beauty to an area for generations.

A new entity has been created in our city — the Charleston Tree Foundation, The purpose of this fund is to make certain that more trees will grace our streets and that pocket parks will begin to beautify spaces that are now barren. People who don't have a chance to plant a tree or who never thought about doing it can have a vehicle for this purpose and can do so forever, since the fund has been established in perpetuity.

This important initiative from the private sector will require funding and work. Tax-deductible checks can be made out to the Charleston Tree Foundation and sent to The Community Foundation, 456 King St., Charleston, 29403. It is hoped that those who participate as well as those who are unable to do so will enjoy the benefits of this effort for years to come.

JOHN WINTHROP
1 NORTH ADGER'S WHARF

The Post and Courier

Friday, May 3, 1996, Letters to the Editor

Pocket parks

As a follow-up to an April 25 edition article, I would like to add that the "pocket parks," a private sector initiative to beautify our city, could not be done without the support of the Parks Department of the city of Charleston.

While our monthly meetings involved raising money and planning the pocket parks that will decorate the northern edge of the city along Highway 17, we often forget that the maintenance of these pocket parks falls upon the taxpayers and the staff who look after our green spaces.

Many people deserve credit for this worthy effort, but most notably the committee members and the representatives of the city who helped every step of the way.

Now the challenge is to add a second park and a third as we approach 1997 and 1998.

JOHN WINTHROP
The Charleston Tree Foundation
1 NORTH ADGER'S WHARF

The Post and Courier

Wednesday, December 11, 1996, Letters to the Editor

Nuclear weapons

It should be a source of inspiration that a growing number of ex-Soviet and American military leaders are promoting the elimination of nuclear weapons. Now that the Cold War is over, it is clear that we need to lead the way in developing a new mindset, a new realization that the greater risk is in going along the path we have traveled over more than 50 years.

Already we are seeing the ambitions of Iraqi and Korean influence others. This can only lead to a less safe world. Our conventional forces are vastly superior to any possible adversary and our competitive edge in technology greater still.

The insurance policy of building a nuclear arsenal has been enormously expensive. Let us lead the way in developing a safer world. It will be a long journey, but we should follow the advice of the wise people suggesting a change in direction in our national defense policy.

JOHN WINTHROP
1 NORTH ADGER'S WHARF

24

The Post and Courier

Friday, April 4, 1997, Letters to the Editor

Don't expand NATO

It is difficult to understand how the advantages of expanding NATO can outweigh the disadvantages.

We have an historic opportunity to reach out to the Russian people — to help them rather than to threaten them — to discourage the leaders from wasting funds on armaments rather than to encourage them — to build confidence rather than distrust.

Before the collapse of the Soviet Union, NATO was an effective and expensive form of insurance to halt the aggressive instincts of the USSR. It might be added that we were lucky to avoid catastrophic conflict.

Now, with Russia attempting to nurture democracy in its most embryonic form, we are sending the wrong signal.

As a grandfather for the first time this year, and as a father of four sons, I want to have hope for the future. My firm conviction is that the spread of democracy and capitalism rather than the spread of NATO and armaments offers the safest path for all of us.

It may be too late to reverse our policy with regard to NATO expansion, but it is never too late to express a thought on such an important matter.

JOHN WINTHROP
1 NORTH ADGER'S WHARF

25

Saturday May 3, 1997, Letters to the Editor

Tree 'renaissance'

The renaissance continues in Charleston. It has a cultural as well as an economic dimension. Historic Charleston's 50th birthday party made us aware of the efforts made to cherish and preserve our past. Looking to the future during this time of vitality and prosperity, we need to consider our open spaces.

The article by Robert Behre in the April 26 *Post and Courier* highlighted the creation of a park along the Septima Clark expressway. Many contributors helped make this dream a reality. A crash effort by the parks department also deserves praise and recognition. The Charleston Tree Foundation has been the vehicle for this accomplishment.

The expansion of parks and trees is an important part of the renaissance in Charleston. It has been noted that trees give shelter to wildlife, they cleanse the air, and they prevent soil and wind erosion. Most importantly, they give our children and grandchildren the hope of quality in their lives; they beautify our living spaces.

The burst of energy and hope released during this time of prosperity in Charleston must be sustained. The planting of trees is only one manifestation of this rising tide, but it offers a chance for all of us to participate. To do so, call Richard Hendry, a member of the Charleston Tree Foundation Committee, at The Community Foundation, 723-3635. Any effort to support this private sector/public sector initiative will be greatly appreciated.

JOHN WINTHROP
1 NORTH ADGER'S WHARF

The Post and Courier

Thursday, September 4, 1997, Letters to the Editor

Mir's benefits

Having visited Soviet Russia in 1956 as part of the first wave of American visitors during the de-Stalinization era, I find the events of recent years astounding.

The degree of cooperation in space travel as well as cultural exchanges, can bring nothing but a sense of relief and hope for the future.

Mir (meaning peace in Russian) has produced far more in the way of scientific accomplishments than many may realize. While the mis-haps may cause embarrassment and even disagreement, this observer feels that we must remember how far we have come since the days we were talking about "an evil empire."

Since my visit, I have always felt that Americans and Russians share basic characteristics — among them a profound sense of curiosity, a basic friendliness and a willingness to work. While the Russian people may enjoy vodka even more then we do, we need to be optimistic and helpful to these people who have suffered so much over the years.

JOHN WINTHROP
1 NORTH ADGER'S WHARF

27

The Post and Courier

Wednesday, November 19, 1997, Letters to the Editor

Travel agents hurt

Travel agents are being short-changed by the airline industry by having their commissions cut by 20 percent, and those of us who have to travel on business are the losers.

Travel agents provide us with a choice: They record our preferences, and they search for the best rates. It is not surprising that 80 percent of travelers prefer to use travel agents.

As an investment adviser, I charge a fee for my services with the hope and understanding that I will add value to our clients' financial picture. If I am honest with myself — indeed, if I am selfishly interested in keeping the travel agency business a healthy business — I should be and will be willing to pay a fee for all the services they provide my firm.

JOHN WINTHROP
1 NORTH ADGER'S WHARF

The Post and Courier

'Moral authority'

It is difficult to conceive a situation where one nation has more conspicuous dominance in so many fields of endeavor as the United States does today.

In the field of technology, America is dominant. In business and commerce, the global reach of such companies as Merck and Microsoft, Coca-Cola and Philip Morris has demonstrated how our advanced skills in marketing and management have given new meaning to industry leadership. Our military strength is awesome.

More troubling is our diminishing moral authority amongst our neighbors. We are still behind on our debt to the United Nations. We cannot seem to understand that the benefits of banning land mines far out-weigh the feeble arguments of those who want them. As champion consumers and formidable polluters, we have not shown restraint.

My hope as a father and grandfather is that we can reflect on these matters during the holiday season. As Americans, we are capable of earning more moral authority.

JOHN WINTHROP
1 NORTH ADGER'S WHARF

The Post and Courier

Monday, March 30, 1998, Letters to the Editor

The controversy over smoking has been creating headlines over the past year. Among the advantages of making our country a healthier place — especially for youngsters — it is also clear a large tax on tobacco would be helpful to the national budget.

Considerably less attention has been directed toward the reduction of gasoline prices during this extended period of moderating inflation. A significant hike in gasoline taxes would help the budget, as well — repairing the roof while the sun is shining as it were.

If we could see positive action taken and some courage among politicians on this subject, we would see a reduction in traffic, improvement in air quality and less dependence on overseas energy supplies as well as further improvement in the budgetary picture. While these are not original thoughts, it seems a uniquely good time to revisit this opportunity — despite the opposition to the idea!

JOHN WINTHROP
1 NORTH ADGER'S WHARF

The Post and Courier

Clinton and China

Human rights deserve our attention. Maintaining contact with the people in the most populated country in the world is vitally important. These two statements do not have to be mutually exclusive. In my judgment President Clinton should represent us and go to China.

Ten years ago a group of us went to China to talk about establishing capital markets. Armed with a Polaroid camera and balloons for mothers and children, as well as reports and speeches for our counterparts, we became impressed by the value of people-to-people contact — just as many others have before and since that memorable trip.

A recent encounter with a student from Shanghai, having graduated magna cum laude from a well known American institution, made me realize once again how important contact between people from different parts of the world is for all of us.

It is possible that I am too biased after establishing a number of solid friendships among the Chinese people, but it is imperative, I believe, that we not be too judgmental abroad when we have a long way to go to get our own house in order.

JOHN WINTHROP
1 NORTH ADGER'S WHARF

Wednesday, July 15, 1998, Letters to the Editor

Sanford kudos

Three cheers for the congressman from the 1st District of South Carolina, Mark Sanford!

By devoting a large portion of his time and effort recently to educating all of us on the importance of correcting and strengthening the Social Security system, he has demonstrated a brand of courage most politicians lack.

Predictably, Rep. Sanford ran into a buzz saw with various politicians from the Northeast at a conference in New England recently. He was making a case for the privatization of the Social Security system.

With each passing month, more of our citizens are learning that privatization of the system with a few other adjustments offers the most secure and compassionate method of solving this very large problem.

Recognizing that self-reliance is central to the American character, we should be proud of our representative and vocal in our support of him, I believe.

JOHN WINTHROP
1 NORTH ADGER'S WHARF

The Post and Courier

Wednesday, August 19, 1998, Letters to the Editor

Preserve open spaces

During the Career administration a number of environmental organizations joined forces to save significant portions of the Alaskan wilderness from commercial interests. Now, with plentiful supplies of energy and no convincing case being made to explore or exploit vast portions of Alaska wilderness in search of petroleum reserves, it appears that a significant portion of this last refuge of wilderness territory will be made available for drilling.

Will we ever learn that as our wideness, our farmland, and our open spaces are reduced, the quality of life of our children and grandchildren will be diminished as a result?

It should be added that America's economic strength will be reduced in the long run if we don't do a better job of protecting this important part of our heritage.

Conservation and environmental awareness make good business sense and good urban planning sense in my opinion. We must do a better job of protecting our precious natural resources.

JOHN WINTHROP
1 NORTH ADGER'S WHARF

33

The Post and Courier

Thursday, November 19, 1998, Letters to the Editor

Global outlook needed

At a recent meeting here in Charleston with a friend from Poland, I was struck by his comment that we are so fortunate, as Americans, to have the Atlantic and Pacific oceans on either side of us. It was easy to understand that comment – particularly since it came from one who was mindful of intrusions from Germany and Russia in years past.

In a world of rapid travel and even more rapid communication, however, it would appear that we may not be so fortunate after all.

The news in the *Post and Courier* as well as on all the primary networks seems increasingly preoccupied with scandal, entertainment and politics rather than Iraq, Honduras and Russia – to name just a few of the trouble spots in today's world.

With John Glenn's journey around planet Earth, we are reminded once again that there are no national boundaries seen from space.

If we are truly the country best equipped at this moment in time to help the world get problems under control, we should become better educated on what is happening beyond our borders – to be more global in our outlook.

This point deserves consideration, I believe, by those delivering the news to us, even though they are driven by commercial interests. National Public Radio is attempting to reverse this trend as it celebrates its 20th birthday.

JOHN WINTHROP
1 NORTH ADGER'S WHARF

34

The Post and Courier

Wednesday, March 31, 1999, Letters to the Editor

Sensible growth

The fuss over Wadmalaw's allowable densities deserves even more attention than it is getting. The Charleston area is such a shining example of splendid living space that people come to this part of our state from all over the country. Indeed, we attract visitors from all over the world – not only because of our historic content but also because of the glory of our wildlife and open spaces.

All of these and other virtues have been made possible because, by and large, the zoning and restrictions we have make sense. Some mistakes have been made in the past, but less so than in other parts of the country.

Recognizing this fact, such young and vital organizations as the American Farmland Trust, one of the most rapid-growing and influential environmental organizations in our country, has included in its agenda a program of planned and sensible growth in urban areas, as well as the preservation of farmland. On a recent visit to Charleston, the president of AFT emphasized this fact.

Our local Coastal Conservation League is fighting the same battle. It is such an important battle to win.

Increasing allowable densities on Wadmalaw would be a big, big mistake in my opinion.

JOHN WINTHROP
1 North Adger's Wharf

35

The Post and Courier

Tuesday, April 27, 1999, Letters to the Editor

Sanford's leadership

What a joy it is to see a politician with integrity! Your April 9 editorial gave a well-deserved salute to Mark Sanford, who has been fighting the battle of fiscal restraint since he first became our congressman. At times this has been an extremely lonely exercise for him.

Approximately eight years ago, a small group assembled periodically here in Charleston to discuss the problem of the mounting federal deficit. Several solutions were offered, but Mark Sanford appropriately realized that meaningful progress can be made only through the political process.

At the time he announced his candidacy, there were many skeptics. During his tenure in Washington, he has become one of the leaders in restoring sanity to the budgetary process, as you indicated. The problem remains with us, but thanks to Rep. Sanford and some others, we may have some hope for the future.

Mark Sanford will be stepping down, as he said he would, but the battle must go on. Let us hope that his successor will be a person of integrity and good judgment, as well.

JOHN WINTHROP
1 NORTH ADGER'S WHARF

The Post and Courier

Wednesday, November 17, 1999, Letters to the Editor

Visit to Russia

Under the leadership of Marshall Goldman, a small group of Americans visited St. Petersburg and Moscow and met with a number of Russian leaders. I was fortunate to be in that group on that trip. Once I returned to Charleston and absorbed my journal, a few conclusions emerged.

Among them: Russia is at a significant crossroads. We need to provide help more with well-educated professionals spending time providing answers to environmental problems, to farm management challenges and to legal enforcement issues. Our mindset has been to throw money at these problems. This policy has been counter-productive.

We must put ourselves in the shoes of our Russian friends — and most of them want to be friends. From their point of view, they have helped Western civilization in World War II, they have helped us disentangle the Serbian problem. At the same time, with all their suffering, they have contributed to the enrichment of life through music and the arts. Our defensive attitude needs fundamental changes.

On the nuclear issue, arms negotiator Paul Nitze and other arms experts have it right. We should unilaterally disarm ourselves of nuclear weapons. They are costly to maintain and do not advance U.S. interests around the world.

Likewise, we need to re-examine the real merits of continuing to expand NATO. By doing so, we are contributing to a situation where Russia feels diminished and humiliated. This policy is misguided.

One voice in the wilderness will never be enough to change what appears to be the backbone of out-dated policy, but at least we should begin to discuss these important matters and speak out, even though others may think we have "lost our grip." A good relationship with Russia is very, very important.

JOHN WINTHROP
1 NORTH ADGER'S WHARF

The Post and Courier

Friday, March 3, 2000, Letters to the Editor

Refresh the spirit

For those of us who tend to be working too hard on a narrow path, let me make a recommendation. Take some time off. Let someone else walk the dogs and take care of any loose ends at home, in the office or with the children. Then take a ride into the country to a place like Milford — located beyond the malls, beyond the sprawl of any city about 90 miles northwest of Charleston.

Constructed more than 160 years ago, this magnificent example of Greek revival architecture reminds the casual visitor of a few things that may be more important than the humdrum activities of our everyday lives.

On this trip that was sponsored by the Friends of the Citadel Library, we were reminded once again of the need to protect our open spaces and to preserve our rich architectural and historic heritage. Milford is one of the rarest and most elegant Greek revival structures in our nation, but there are a number of other plantation homes open to the public in our state as well.

Both farmland and magnificent old houses are being replaced all too rapidly by malls and housing developments. (Between 1987 and 1992, America lost 15 percent of its open farmland.) This visit to Mr. Jenrette's plantation retreat refreshed the spirit and snapped a few things into perspective for at least one deskbound environmentalist.

JOHN WINTHROP
1 NORTH ADGER'S WHARF

The Post and Courier

Tuesday, April 4, 2000, Letters to the Editor

The Omega Project

A very interesting event took place in Columbia recently — a conference on racial understanding sponsored by the Palmetto Project. Many of those who attended left with the conviction that if those of different racial origins and backgrounds sat down with each other in a systematic, organized way, the results could be very positive.

This effort, already under way in many parts of our state under the supervision of the Palmetto Project, is called the "Omega Project." The success of this concept in various pockets of our state explains the fact that mutual interests, cutting across cultural and racial barriers, have resulted in mutual sympathy and understanding, if not racial harmony.

This is a mere ray of hope which needs broadcasting in a state that is too often known for the flag issue or the well-publicized problems of The Citadel. The idea of the Omega Project can and should be replicated beyond our borders.

The Palmetto Project is beginning to make a difference. The conference in Columbia ("Imagine South Carolina") punctuated this reality and provided momentum to the Omega Project.

JOHN WINTHROP
1 NORTH ADGER'S WHARF

39

The Post and Courier

Plant trees

As a long-term tree farmer (over 30 years) and active environmentalist, I was encouraged by the government's proposal to encourage the planting of trees to reduce global warming.

It should be remembered that, in addition to helping in the battle to reduce global winning, trees prevent soil erosion and provide habitat for wildlife. They also improve the quality of our own lives and beautify the planet.

My family's adventure in tree farming is a happy one. Our property on the Savannah River is incorporated and my older sons serve as directors. I serve as chairman until I'm fired. Our stated objectives are to improve the environment, to add value, and to have fun.

JOHN WINTHROP
1 NORTH ADGER'S WHARF

ℭhe ℘ost and ℭourier

Sunday, October 29, 2000, Letters to the Editor

A broader view

Something positive seems to be happening in the presentation of the news over this past month amid all the bloodshed and horror associated with the turmoil in the Mideast.

The breakdown of the peace process, coincident with the change of leadership in Serbia has, by necessity, elevated our awareness of the importance of what is going on in the rest of the world, A higher level of focus on foreign policy in the presidential debates has echoed this development as well.

If only the trend could continue so that we could learn more about the complexities of the world — and perhaps even the need to get along with one another. These substantive issues seem a bit more important than so much of the sports-related, theater-related, scandal-related junk dished up by the media.

JOHN WINTHROP
1 NORTH ADGER'S WHARF

The Post and Courier

Tuesday, January 30, 2001, Letters to the Editor

Protect quality of life

Many who have studied economics are familiar with the concept of "regional specialization." Each country, each city, each region has come to understand intuitively, if not by design, what attributes distinguish it from others. Our country has led the world in management skills and high technology. Parts of the Southeast have become a timber basket and a tourist Mecca.

By the same logic, we can say that our part of South Carolina — and most particularly Charleston — has become known as a destination for those seeking quality of life without overloading our infrastructure and facilities.

This community will prosper so long as we protect our primary asset — just as the country and our region must define and safeguard all that defines our unique quality.

Clearly the expansion of the port facility will put a huge burden on our road system, increase pollution, and impact the quality of life in Charleston, a community that has already demonstrated its ability to attract a diversity of "new economy" activities that have fostered prosperity over the past decade.

More voices of reason need to be heard on this important issue.

JOHN WINTHROP
1 NORTH ADGER'S WHARF

42

Thursday, May 24, 2001, Letters to the Editor

Isolationist drift

There is much to be concerned about in the drift toward isolationism.

Most objective observers would agree that the global nature of environmental problems as well as the economic inter-dependence among nations demands a need for greater understanding and cooperation among the people inhabiting planet Earth.

These realities point toward the requirement of supporting the United Nations and reaching for a better understanding of how the world works — environmentally, economically and even spiritually. This plea is written on the desk of a registered Republican.

JOHN WINTHROP
1 NORTH ADGER'S WHARF

The Post and Courier

Sunday, September 23, 2001, Letters to the Editor

An opportunity

As we recover from the shocking events of September 11, it appears to some of us that we may now have an extraordinary opportunity, in geopolitical terms, of forging a global alliance — despite the fragile economy, and despite all the hazards of fighting an enemy who lurks in the shadows.

There are likely to be stark choices ahead of us in terms of the sacrifices we are willing to make. There are also decisions ahead for the leaders of various countries who must make some difficult choices as well.

As we build our coalition and develop a convincing strategy to combat terrorists — all of it in the framework of biochemical and nuclear threats — we may be able to make positive steps toward international cooperation.

If so, the foundation will be stronger for building a global economy.

We have no choice but to lead in this daunting task, given the political and economic realities of our present situation. May God give us both strength and wisdom as we embark upon this effort!

JOHN WINTHROP
1 NORTH ADGER'S WHARF

Haunting attack

News of the unthinkable horror in New York reached me in Boston while in the middle of an investment meeting. We had just completed a peaceful breakfast at the Boston Harbor Hotel, admiring the boats, the blue sky and the airplanes leaving Logan Airport. As we vacated the building, we knew nothing about the connection between Logan Airport and the Twin Towers horror.

Now, nearly two months later, many of us are haunted by the idea of our beloved country brought to its knees by a group of people we do not understand. The vision of the destruction of our communication and travel systems, of our water and energy supplies, of our computer and technology apparatus — all of these nightmares — leave some of us a bit disoriented.

However, there are some other reflections worth noting. Some of us feel compelled to refocus on those things that really matter:
- We reach to a higher power for inspiration and a better understanding of our condition.
- We fly the American flag with greater enthusiasm than ever before.
- We appreciate the hard work and sacrifices of so many who have made America what it is today.
- We want to hug our children and grandchildren and thank those of past generations who are no longer with us.

- We find David McCullough's book on John Adams and other such literary works take on new meaning.

It may be a bit optimistic in light of the circumstances and threats surrounding us, but it would appear that the United States has a unique opportunity to create better understanding among many countries as we attempt to build a global alliance against terrorism.

As we re-examine our own assumptions and values, we may find ourselves better able to reach out with less arrogance and more of a spirit of compromise to those who want to be our friends.

If we are successful, we will find that we are building a more solid foundation — not only for eliminating terrorism, but also in building a stronger global economy.

In any event, given the economic and political realities of today, we have no choice but to lead in this daunting task. May God give us the strength, the patience and the wisdom as we go down this road.

JOHN WINTHROP
1 NORTH ADGER'S WHARF

The Post and Courier

Russian alliance

The battle against terrorism has given new impetus to the need to create a stronger alliance with Russia. In my view, this is long overdue.

In the past the Soviets helped us win World War II more than is generally recognized in our history books. More recently, Russia helped "pull our chestnuts out of the fire" in the former Yugoslavia. Now we are finding common cause in the war against terrorism.

Three trips to that part of the world reinforced my conviction that we need to forge stronger ties with the people of Russia — not just for a source of energy and help against terrorists, but also because the people of that long-suffering land need our help as they work out developing their brand of democracy in a constructive way.

It was clear as far back as 1956, when a college classmate and I visited five Soviet cities, that we had far more in common with the people we met in a number of cities on a two-week voyage than we had ever anticipated.

JOHN WINTHROP
1 NORTH ADGER'S WHARF

The Post and Courier

Thursday, May 30, 2002, Letters to the Editor

Angel Oak important

Occasionally, a father should be allowed to provide a word of praise for his sons. This thought was triggered by the lead editorial in a recent *Post and Courier*, which stressed the importance of preserving the land surrounding the Angel Oak.

Historic Tree Preservation has just completed important work on the Angel Oak to ensure the survival of that famous tree. Limbs were removed; cables were installed as needed; and a commitment was made by HTP for annual inspections to assure the health of die Angel Oak. My son, Gren, founder and president of Historic Tree Preservation, has long been an avid environmentalist and conservationist.

Now, the large job of securing easements on the land around the Angel Oak remains. American Farmland Trust, along with help from local conservation groups will back this effort. My oldest son, John Jr. ("Jay"), serves on the Trust's board. That national board is in the process of establishing an office in the Southeast, which can provide those interested in land preservation with a valuable resource. My sons make me so proud. Environmental causes are so important.

JOHN WINTHROP
1 NORTH ADGER'S WHARF

—— The Post and Courier ——

Saturday, June 15, 2002, Letters to the Editor

Sanford's Showing

Mark Sanford's show of strength in the GOP runoff for governor is noteworthy.

It is noteworthy not just because he is an outstanding citizen of our part of the state, not just because he was more gracious in his victory speech, and not just because he established a fine record as a congressman.

More importantly, Mark is a man of integrity. Whether or not we agree with him on every issue, it is comforting to know that public service continues to attract a few people who will make every effort to do what they say they will do.

Many of us feel that Mark is that kind of man. In today's world, these qualities are rarely found.

JOHN WINTHROP
1 NORTH ADGER'S WHARF

The Post and Courier

Saturday, September 16, 2002, Letters to the Editor

Cuban sanctions

Often our elected leaders do not lead us. Women are now an important contributing segment of our workforce; the Vietnam War came to an end eventually, thus saving more lives and treasure. Both major events began with a grassroots effort and are only two examples of democratically elected officials finding new direction — leadership from the bottom up!

It might be argued today, with the possibility of a war with Iraq in the headlines almost daily, that we should pause to consider the debate more in cost /benefit terms. Without popular backing at home and without our allies backing us, the cost of ousting Saddam Hussein will be far greater than initially anticipated.

In like manner, the human and financial cost of keeping sanctions in place has accelerated. It is just possible that with investment in diplomacy, intelligence and more complete education about those parts of the world we feel threaten us, more benefits may be realized.

Let us not forget that with the Communist menace less obvious now, that sanctions against Cuba seem untidy at best.

JOHN WINTHROP
1 NORTH ADGER'S WHARF

The Post and Courier

Monday, October 21, 2002, Letters to the Editor

New Gibbes' director

What A fine introduction Dottie Ashley gave us to Betsy Fleming, the new director of the Gibbes. The High Profile article outlined and described a woman with a brain and common sense as well as beauty and strong people skills.

The Gibbes is certain to benefit from this rare woman with Southern roots and a strong educational background. Reaching out to those parts of our community as well as establishing partnerships with other cultural institutions will be high on Ms. Fleming's agenda. Even more important, her attitude and enthusiasm wilt add greatly to these and other initiatives. Power to your hand, Betsy. I can understand why your friends boast about you.

JOHN WINTHROP
1 NORTH ADGER'S WHARF

The Post and Courier

date unknown, Letters to the Editor

Questions on Iraq

Every day there is news about Iraq. And every day many of us are haunted by the question of whether an appropriate cost/benefit analysis has been conducted by those in charge. It is too late to question whether we should have transformed Saddam's army into a police force rather than into a police force rather than into an unemployed mass of angry people. It is too late to question whether we should have placed a higher priority on protecting the archaeological treasures in Baghdad.

Today, the questions that must be asked are: When do we lose our credibility as we attempt to identify the source of weapons of mass destruction elsewhere? At what point do we appear to be so arrogant that our allies desert us? Can we afford to act unilaterally and preemptively in an increasingly hostile world?

We constitute only 5 percent of the world's population. Some of us feel we should be thinking hard about these different foreign policy questions.

Many observers of our foreign policy share several concerns.

Among them:

- We many not have conducted an appropriate cost/benefit analysis before confronting our adversaries.

- We may not appear to care about the views of our potential allies.

- We may appear too often to be materialistic, too arrogant and too dependant on our military force.

We live in a dangerous time. Perhaps it is a good idea to examine the impression we are making abroad more than we have. Perhaps we should move away from terrifying unilateralism and toward a more enlightened diplomacy.

Such adjustment is needed, I submit, in dealing with environmental problems, military strategy and even with terrorism.

JOHN WINTHROP
1 NORTH ADGER'S WHARF

The Post and Courier

Friday, January 16, 2004, Letters to the Editor

Waste and gluttony

With the federal deficit quietly creating more of a problem for our children and grandchildren each day, we can take some comfort in the fact that restoring health to our state budget has assumed high priority for the Sanford administration in Columbia.

A combination of spending cuts and the sale of assets should allow us to retain essential services and restore hope for our state's financial health. In contrast, we see little evidence of fiscal discipline at the federal level. It is always easier to think of ways to spend more — particularly in an election year — rather than to face up to the long-term problems, most particularly the rising costs, of Medicare and Social Security.

The storm clouds are on the horizon. Mark Sanford understands this fact, as do a few other governors. Perhaps key members of both parties in Washington should take a moment to study and understand the consequences of waste and gluttony on the fiscal chessboard.

JOHN WINTHROP
1 NORTH ADGER'S WHARF

The Post and Courier

Tuesday, March 30, 2004, Letters to the Editor

Flag repair

Robert Behre's article describing the return of the flag that flew over Castle Pinckney 143 years ago was heartwarming, especially for a transplant from Massachusetts. Long before the War Between the States, there were close ties between Boston and Charleston. Indeed, the oldest club at Harvard College has records of the bonds that existed among its members many years ago.

While the repair of the flag is proving to be a very costly burden for the South Carolina Historical Society, the healing this gesture symbolizes is worth far more than the dollars spent. My only regret is that the ceremony of repatriation had to wait so long.

JOHN WINTHROP
1 NORTH ADGER'S WHARF

The Post and Courier

Thursday, June 3, 2004, Letters to the Editor

Salute to Sanford

Somewhere along the way, we seem to have "lost our grip" in coming to terms with budget deficits. On a state level, Mark Sanford deserves far more support than he got from his Legislature while trying to restore integrity to the finances of South Carolina. There are few politicians who are willing to cut back on unnecessary expenses.

On a national level, it must be said that belt-tightening is urgently needed. Budget deficits are capable of causing more damage than terrorists. The higher interest rates climb — a likely result of the "crowding out" problem as the demand for funds rises with higher deficits — the more likely inflation will take hold with a vengeance. Inflation is the financial equivalent of cancer, in my judgment.

These thoughts are not popular, but it is clear that many of our elected leaders should be given a primer course in economics. We need the help of government at all levels.

Gov. Sanford should be given a salute for his attempt to correct this problem in the Palmetto State.

JOHN WINTHROP
1 NORTH ADGER'S WHARF

Storm surprise

We thought a trip to Orlando would be a breeze — three full days visiting colleges with my youngest son! What could be better? We made our college visits brief just before the oncoming storm changed direction. On Friday. August 13, we found ourselves in the eye of the worst hurricane to hit Florida this century. Our building shook; water came into our room; trees were uprooted, and the American flag outside was ripped in the fierce winds.

With the airport in Orlando damaged and flights cancelled, we drove back to Charleston the following day, mission accomplished! But clearly the overriding impression was one of joy upon returning to the Holy City, along with admiration for all those bringing supplies and repair equipment to those less fortunate. Both Hugo and Charley packed a mighty punch.

JOHN WINTHROP
1 NORTH ADGER'S WHARF

— **The Post and Courier** —

Thursday, October 28, 2004, Letters to the Editor

Red Sox and all's well

Untangling the mess in Iraq, restoring fiscal sanity in Washington and baiting the degradation of the environment are serious problems.

These issues are not to be underestimated.

However, seeing the Red Sox and Patriots win allows us to believe God is alive and well.

Let's not speak while the flavor lasts.

JOHN WINTHROP
1 NORTH ADGER'S WHARF

The Post and Courier

Friday, December 17, 2004, Letters to the Editor

Show of Courage

It seems odd to call Sen. Lindsey Graham "the senior senator" from South Carolina, but already he has assumed considerable stature. By speaking out clearly on such matters as prisoner scandals and the need to restrain the undisciplined spending problem of our government, he has demonstrated considerable courage.

Now he is facing the Social Security dilemma by asking for sacrifice and deserves support. Those of us who have children and grandchildren need to be clear about the burden we are placing on future generations. We must urge elected leaders to show the courage that is becoming the hallmark of our new senior senator.

JOHN WINTHROP
1 NORTH ADGER'S WHARF

The Post and Courier

Cost cutting

As a registered Republican and long-time friend and supporter of our governor, I was disturbed to read about the initiative to eliminate the Salkehatchie University, a South Carolina campus in Walterboro and Allendale.

Not only does the education of local youngsters add to the talent pool in the area, but education in any location has a multiplier effect in assisting the community. Allendale and Walterboro are in serious need of any spark of economic vitality. The campus in both areas, particularly in Allendale, has provided much needed economic support in the past and, by educating young men and women, it promises more benefits to the surrounding area in the future. In fact, any serious cost/benefit analysis demands nurturing these productive educational centers rather than being critical of them.

Let's think about other ways of cutting costs and/or increasing revenues for the State.

JOHN WINTHROP
1 NORTH ADGER'S WHARF

The Post and Courier

Friday, May 6, 2005, Letters to the Editor

Reckless spending

If the lack of fiscal discipline is a concern to us, what should we do? Contact our representative? Discuss the problem with friends, or write a letter to the editor?

I am attempting to do all three. As a grandfather, I am both concerned and a bit angry ... concerned because the budget gap is not even close to getting under control and angry because the current administration and many of our leaders in Washington do not give it the priority it deserves.

Budget deficits with the very real possibility of inflation gaining momentum can cause a major problem for future generations of Americans.

Spending at the federal level has not been so out of control in over 30 years, and the entitlement challenges of Medicare and Social Security present problems that all but a few of our selected representatives have the courage to face.

JOHN WINTHROP
1 NORTH ADGER'S WHARF

The Post and Courier

A final salute

Gen. William Westmoreland and I planted a tree on Tradd Street together. That is how we first met. I was a Yankee newcomer; he was an established South Carolinian. He had led our troops with bravery and honor; I had been an anti-war activist many years ago.

We bonded early as neighbors but Kitsy, with her generosity, wonderful hospitality and warmth, cemented the relationship as she has with so many admirers here in Charleston. Their children and grandchildren bonded with us as well. What a man! What a marriage! What a family! What a loss!

JOHN WINTHROP
1 NORTH ADGER'S WHARF

The Post and Courier

Saturday, October 1, 2005, Letters to the Editor

Wake-up call

It seems everyone is complaining about the spike in gasoline prices.

Is it possible that the hurricanes are doing what the politicians have never had the courage to put in place — a conservation tax on gas at the pump?

Could the results of higher prices: give us a wake-up call on the urgent need to find alternative fuels to satisfy our addictions, and ease some of the traffic burdens nationwide and improve the environment? At least some of these questions need to be answered. These problems beg for a solution.

JOHN WINTHROP
1 NORTH ADGER'S WHARF

The Post and Courier

Thursday, August 3, 2006, Letters to the Editor

New world

During these dark days in the Middle East and around the world (when some believe we may be in the early stages of World War III), it would be interesting to see what our reaction would be if our Heavenly Father appeared on the early morning news with this message:

"Your foreign policy does not appear to be working very well. In fact, you may be creating more terrorists than you are killing; America's moral authority is declining and may be leading to reduced influence around the world; your addiction to gasoline and fossil fuels seems to be degrading the planet and spending by your officials appears to be out of control.

"For starters, consider reacting with generosity toward your enemies; give more aid to those countries less fortunate than your own; mandate a gasoline tax gradually; pass a law requiring a balanced budget in Washington; and try to put a higher priority on the environmental protection of the planet with the proceeds of the gasoline tax."

How would we react? Could we understand that we are entering new world with new rules on warfare, diplomacy and the environment? Can we begin to look at these serious problems in a new way? Do we have the capacity to change directions?

JOHN WINTHROP
1 NORTH ADGER'S WHARF